3:16

A STUDY
FOR
SMALL GROUPS

MAX LUCADO

THOMAS NELSON
Since 1798

NASHVILLE   DALLAS   MEXICO CITY   RIO DE JANEIRO   BEIJING

Published in Nashville, Tennessee by Thomas Nelson. Thomas Nelson is a trademark of Thomas Nelson, Inc.

Thomas Nelson, Inc. titles may be purchased in bulk for educational, business, fundraising, or sales promotional use. For information, please e-mail SpecialMarkets@ThomasNelson.com.

ISBN-10: 1-4185-2923-0
ISBN-13: 978-1-4185-2923-9

Printed in the United States of America
08 09 10 RRD 6

CONTENTS

1

THE MOST FAMOUS CONVERSATION IN THE BIBLE

SCRIPTURE FOCUS:
John 3:1–12

LESSON OBJECTIVE:
To discover that real life can only be found in a faith relationship
with Jesus Christ and to commit to living within that relationship.

*"For God so loved the world that
he gave his one and only Son,
that whoever believes in him
shall not perish but have eternal life"*
(John 3:16).

REWIND

Nicodemus had to visit Jesus in secret. After all, he was a prominent Jewish leader, a member of the Pharisees. This was the group that had investigated John the Baptist and was now building a case against Jesus. Nicodemus, however, abandoned his role as a prosecutor in order to seek personal answers. Nicodemus knew enough to make him wonder if Jesus really was the fulfillment of the prophecy that was central to the Jewish faith. His colleagues weren't convinced, but Nicodemus was intrigued.

Even though he was curious, Nicodemus reserved judgment. He misunderstood Jesus's words about the new birth. He couldn't seem to grasp the idea that life change is a God-thing; he believed that God could be found in keeping the law and doing the right things. Heaven—for Nicodemus, the Pharisees, and traditionalists—was something to be earned. Jesus offered what Nicodemus was seeking; Nicodemus just wasn't so sure about Jesus's plan.

RETHINK

Your doubts about a faith-based relationship might not be the same as those Nicodemus had. Maybe you wonder if God really cares for you as much as the Bible says he does. Maybe you question God's willingness and desire to intervene in the problems you are facing. For you, salvation might be nothing more than insurance against spending an eternity in hell; it has no present value. Nicodemus tried religion and found it empty. You might be in the same situation.

What, other than faith, have you tried in order to make sense out of life? (Check all that apply.)

_____ *religion*

_____ *relationships*

_____ *the pursuit of prosperity*

_____ *possessions*

_____ *popularity*

_____ *philosophy*

_____ *power*

_____ *other:*

Describe how you discovered your solution(s) wasn't working.

Complete Nicodemus's statement from your own perspective. "Jesus, I've heard about your works and

_____

_____ *."*

Nicodemus had religious credentials that he thought were enough. He worked for a religious organization, spoke the religious language, and participated in religious activities. He might not have been the best person in the world, but he certainly wasn't the worst. He was in good standing with God . . . or was he?

Jesus told Nicodemus that being good wasn't good enough. Even being religious wouldn't make it possible for Nicodemus to understand what Jesus was talking about. Even though Nicodemus thought he had the spiritual life under control, he was missing the main ingredient—he had never been born again.

> *Describe the time when you were "born again." Where were you? Who was there? What was the experience like?*

What does it mean if you don't remember being born again? It means you might be suffering from Nicodemusitis—the misconception that a person can earn eternal life. You don't earn it. You can't purchase it. You don't get into heaven as part of the family plan. This way of thinking might be new to you; it was new to Nicodemus.

Nicodemus was a professional questioner. He took everything literally. When Jesus said that a person must be born again, Nicodemus was quick to jump on the literal impossibility of such an idea. The Pharisees were good at that.

Some of us would make good Pharisees because we tend to overlook the spiritual significance of biblical instructions, choosing instead to nitpick the minutia. Like defense attorneys, we badger the prosecution's witness, hoping to poke holes in the testimony. If we can just find one loophole, then that instruction won't apply to us.

What do you think pops into the minds of non-spiritual people when they hear the words "born again"?
_____ *physical rebirth*
_____ *spiritual rebirth*
_____ *religious nonsense*
_____ *total confusion*

If someone asked you to explain what it means to be "born again" in everyday words, what would you say?

REFLECT

When Jesus suggested that Nicodemus needed to be born again, he implied something specific—Nicodemus needed to be born from above. Nicodemus was powerless; he had to allow God to do something in his life.

Why is it so hard for some people to allow God to work in their lives?

What has prevented you from allowing God to work in your life?

This conversation with Nicodemus leads to what many believe is the most important verse in the entire Bible. People who have hardly read a word of Scripture even know the words in this verse.

Fill in the blanks:
For _____ so loved the _____ that he gave his one and only _____, that whoever believes in him shall not _____ but have _____ life.

It is interesting to look at two contrasts in this verse: God—world; eternal—perish. This is the contrast that resonates throughout Scripture. The world's ways cause us to perish; God's ways lead us to eternal life. There is no other way to obtain eternal life. This single verse of Scripture offers several unbelievable truths—truths that we often find hard to grasp.

In the space beside each phrase, write what that phrase means to your spiritual life.
1. God so loved -

2. that He gave His one and only Son -

3. shall not perish but have eternal life -

Maybe this is the first time you've thought about it in this way. Many of us read through that verse without thinking much about its meaning to our lives. Yet this verse sums up the very core of our faith. Without a thorough understanding of the truths in this verse, our faith will be built on a weak foundation.

REACT

Read John 19:38–42. Nicodemus was a changed man. He initially encountered Jesus secretly, but he later took a bold stand for Jesus in a society that was hostile toward Jesus and his followers. The disciples were in hiding when Joseph of Arimathea and Nicodemus claimed Jesus's body and prepared it for burial.

How has your faith changed you? In what ways are you taking a stand for Jesus?

What are some of the situations in which you, like the disciples, hide your relationship with God?

How do you think God feels when those who claim to love him hide their faith? (Mark all that apply.)

_____ *He is thrilled.*
_____ *He understands.*
_____ *He is heart-broken.*
_____ *People of faith never hide their faith.*

Later, Nicodemus would be able to explain what it means to be born again. Not because he studied it, but because he experienced it. When it comes to your faith, are you studying it or are you experiencing it?

2

NO ONE LIKE HIM

SCRIPTURE FOCUS:
Isaiah 40:18–31

LESSON OBJECTIVE:
To discover that God is in the midst of every
detail of life—no matter how small—and to
commit to trusting him in every situation.

*"To whom, then, will you compare God?
What image will you compare him to?"*
(Isaiah 40:18)

REWIND

In the book of Isaiah, chapters 40–55 are directed to the Israelites in the early days of their Babylonian captivity. With the glory of David's kingdom and Solomon's temple existing only in their memories, the people lamented their situation. Why were the people in captivity? The answer to that question is a long one, but the generalized reason was their persistent rebellion against God. How had the people rebelled against God? For one, they had abandoned authentic worship in favor of idol worship.

Why would God's people abandon him and pursue worship of meaningless idols? Maybe they were bored or wanted change. Maybe the social pressures were too great. Maybe they got mad at God because he didn't deliver what they wanted according to their schedules. It sounds familiar, doesn't it?

RETHINK

Have you ever asked God, "Why me?" or "Why now?" You might have said it in a different way, but we all have wondered about God's timing and purpose for some events in our lives. Sometimes we aren't very good at connecting our actions with the consequences we experience. We repeatedly disobey, only to question God when we find ourselves square in the middle of the consequences of our disobedience.

> *Think about a situation in which you have disobeyed*
> *God's prompting or biblical instructions. In the space*
> *below, describe how you responded to God when you began*
> *experiencing the consequences of your disobedience.*

Isaiah asks his audience to identify anything that was comparable to God. He specifically asks if God can be compared to an idol made by a craftsman, covered in gold, and adorned with silver. This was the type of idol worshiped by the wealthy in society. The poor people were left to carve their idols from wood. Each socioeconomic group in the culture had its own type of idol.

> *What are some of the ways in which we disappoint God*
> *today? What makes these actions or thoughts so appealing?*

Maybe some of the Israelites thought God had forgotten them. They felt insignificant and unimportant in the grand scheme of things. We can relate, can't we? When life turns upside down, we must be reminded of the fact that God indeed is in control and that he cares for us.

> *What are some of the evidences of God's existence that you experience on a regular basis?*
>
> | | | |
> |---|---|---|
> | _____ sun | _____ moon | _____ stars |
> | _____ rain | _____ wind | _____ seasons |
> | _____ love | _____ provision | _____ breath |
> | _____ healing | _____ compassion | _____ laughter |

The very presence of a moral code is evidence of God's existence and concern for every area of our lives. Right and wrong are wired into our makeup long before we understand what they are. People who refuse to acknowledge God have the ability to identify and publicize injustice. Why? Because God implanted that ability in us. The fact that we know what injustice *is* testifies to the fact that God exists.

The existence of a car forces us to believe there is an assembly plant and designer, even though we've never seen either one. When you turn on your television, you know that there was both an inventor and a manufacturer behind its creation, though you've never met the inventor nor toured the plant.

> *What do the clouds, stars, sun, moon, tide, wind, seasons, rain, and snow lead us to believe?*

Can we accept these normal elements of life and ignore the existence of an inventor and a master plan? Only if we have pre-determined to deny God's existence.

REFLECT

Read Isaiah 40:18–31. God was disrespected by his followers. They ignored the obvious and chose to worship inanimate objects rather than the living God. It was as if they were speaking about the artist while standing in front of his canvas, his paintbrush in his hand and his pallet still wet. In admiring the work, they complimented something that lacked the ability to create such a work of art rather than complimenting the artist. The artist would be incensed; God likewise.

In this passage, God seems appalled that the Israelites could experience all they had been through and yet turn to idols rather than the Creator. They knew the stories of the crossing of the Red Sea and David and Goliath. They had seen God do incredible things in their lives, yet they ignored him. Now they were whining because they were suffering the consequences of their actions.

When was the last time you whined to God? In retrospect, was whining the best option? Why or why not?

The words of John echo through our deepest valleys . . . "For God so loved!" We can hear those words when we are on the highest peaks. There is nowhere we can go to escape this undeniable truth. Creation proves it to be true. John didn't question God's existence; he stated it as a foundational, non-negotiable fact.

John knew that God was real because he had tangible proof. Read the following Scriptures and identify the proof within each verse.

Psalm 19:1

Psalm 74:16

Psalm 90:2

Psalm 97:6

Isaiah 46:9

John 5:26

Acts 17:25

James 1:13

REACT

There really is no one like God. Scripture is one of the ways in which God reveals himself. Nature is another. Evidence is all around us to prove that God is alive and well. Because he exists, we can be sure he is in control.

What is one situation that you want to give to God right now?

How has this situation been affecting your life?

When we look back at the lives of some of the biblical writers, we understand that they wrote more from their experiences than their education. Several of the psalms reflect David's personal ups and downs. In the New Testament, we read about Paul's ongoing struggle between his old nature and his new nature. That's why God gave us his Word—so you and I will have a reliable source of wisdom for dealing with everyday life. God loves us that much and more!

15

Life at times appears to fall to pieces; it seems irreparable. But it's going to be okay. How can you know? Because *God* so loved the world. And,

Since he has no needs, you cannot tire him.
Since he is without age, you cannot lose him.
Since he has no sin, you cannot corrupt him.

3

HOPE FOR THE HARD HEART

SCRIPTURE FOCUS:

Exodus 32:1–35

LESSON OBJECTIVE:

To discover the sources of a hardened heart and to commit to
renewing a vibrant relationship with God.

*"I have seen these people," the LORD said to
Moses, "and they are a stiff-necked people."*
(Exodus 32:9).

REWIND

Three months after escaping Egypt, the Israelites arrived at Mount Sinai (Horeb) with their memories of the spectacular crossing of the Red Sea. The miraculous crossing reminded them that God was indeed special, since the same sea that allowed their crossing on dry land swallowed up pharaoh and his chariots. Their celebration on the eastern shore of the Red Sea was definitely a celebration of praise. They headed southeast toward Mount Sinai because Moses had been instructed not to head northeast through Philistia (Exodus 13:17). Through a series of miracles, God demonstrated to the Israelites his power and presence. Upon arrival at Mount Sinai, Moses ascended the mountain for instructions from God (Exodus 19). He was told to remind the people of what God had done on their behalf and what had happened to the Egyptians who opposed him. The people were in agreement—God had proven himself to them. In Exodus 20, the Ten Commandments were given to the Israelites. These instructions regulated the relationships between God's people and God and between God's people and themselves. God followed these instructions with regulations that applied to almost every area of life. Moses's extended stay on the mountain tested the patience of the Israelites who thought that their journey to the Promised Land would be a short one. Their memories of God's actions on their behalf faded and they began to grumble and complain.

RETHINK

A hardened heart is not uncommon today. It can happen to anyone, regardless of his or her personal or spiritual strength. A hardened heart is evidence of a spiritual problem. That's what happened to the Israelites; that's what happens to us.

> *Describe the last time you experienced a hardened heart. What caused it?*

The Israelites grew spiritually impatient. They didn't want to wait for Moses to return from his meeting with God; they didn't want to waste time on their way to the Promised Land. We have the same problem—we grow impatient when God doesn't do things according to our schedules. We get angry when we don't understand why the journey is taking so long. We begin to question God's love for us. We say, "Maybe God loves some people, but he obviously doesn't love me."

> *Describe a time when you have been impatient with God. How did your impatience affect your spiritual life?*

John 3:16 tells us that "God so loved *the world* . . . ." That's an all-inclusive statement that we often overlook. The Israelites made the mistake of believing that God's love was limited to those he favored. We often conclude that some people have God's favor while others don't. We easily forget what God has done for us in the past and begin feeling sorry for ourselves.

How often do you have spiritual self-pity parties?
____ *not at all*
____ *once a year*
____ *monthly*
____ *weekly*
____ *daily*
____ *constantly*

What are three things God has done for you in the past that can serve as reminders of his love for you?
1.

2.

3.

The Israelites wanted a god they could see and touch; we can easily fall into the same way of thinking. They melted their valuables and fashioned a golden calf; we trade what really matters for modern-day idols—possessions, appearance, popularity, wealth, and even religion.

Maybe you've never melted your jewelry to make a golden calf, but you might have allowed something in your life to become more important than your relationship with God. What are some of those things that have displaced God in your life?

REFLECT

Read Exodus 32:1–35. The calf wasn't just a convenient image to worship; it was reminiscent of the cow and the bull that were part of Egyptian worship rituals. The bull also was part of the Baal worship of the Canaanite culture. The Israelites watered down their faith by including elements of other religious practices. Something they thought would strengthen their faith actually weakened it.

Have you ever done something you thought would make you spiritually stronger and later discovered that it actually weakened your faith? If so, what was it and how did you overcome it?

Why did the Israelites make such a tragic mistake? In a word, they were afraid. Being afraid isn't an offense to God, but how we respond to our fears can be a problem. When the Israelites were scared, they reverted to something in their past. Even though they had been slaves in Egypt, life back then was predictable. Like the Israelites, when we are scared, we seek out the most recent stability . . . even if that stability is negative.

Place an X on the continuum below representing your level of spiritual fear.

Calm————————————————————*Panicked*

About what are you most fearful?
____ *your past*
____ *your present*
____ *your future*

The end of the story of the golden calf is more tragic than its beginning. The people were permanently affected by their decision to turn their backs on God. According to verse 35, the people were plagued because of what they did.

REACT

The Israelites probably had a series of "if only" moments. If only they had remained faithful to God. If only they had resisted the urge to worship the golden calf. If only they had waited patiently for the Lord. If only . . .

What is one "if only" moment you've had in your life?

In what ways have you experienced the consequences of the bad decision you made?

The bad news is that we often live with the consequences of our sins. The good news is that God is the God of forgiveness and restoration. We can be in a right relationship with God even after we have let Him down. We can move forward, leaving the mistakes of the past behind us.

In the space provided, write a prayer confessing those things that have separated you from God. Then ask him for forgiveness and for a fresh start.

Read Psalm 71:14–15. Read this passage again as a personal declaration of your attitude toward life. By daily remembering what God has done for you in the past, you will become more and more resistant to developing a hardened heart.

4

WHEN YOU GET BOOTED OUT

SCRIPTURE FOCUS:
Hosea 3:1–5

LESSON OBJECTIVE:
To discover God's relentless love and commit to living
in a right relationship with our heavenly Father.

"Then the LORD said to me, 'Go again,
love a woman who is loved by a lover
and is committing adultery,
just like the love of the LORD for the
children of Israel, who look to other gods
and love the raisin cakes of the pagans'"
(Hosea 3:1 NKJV).

REWIND

The book of Hosea has been described as one of the more unusual books in the Bible. As a prophet, Hosea lived through one of the most difficult object lessons we can imagine. Hosea was told to marry a woman who would be unfaithful to him—a sin that was punishable by death. Gomer, Hosea's wife, personified the attitude of the Israelites toward God. Their three children would be given names that reminded the Israelites of God's displeasure with them. Gomer's actions resulted in her being enslaved. But God instructed Hosea to pay a price to redeem her—a picture of God's desire to redeem his people from their sin.

RETHINK

God wouldn't have to look very hard to find reasons to stop loving us. However, in spite of the countless reasons, he refuses to end his pursuit of us. God's pursuit isn't motivated by his desire to punish us; no, it is motivated by his desire to love us.

> *In what ways do you see evidence of God's love in your daily life?*
>
>
> *Why does God want to have a relationship with you?*
> _____ *to make your life miserable*
> _____ *to provide rules and regulations*
> _____ *because He needs you*
> _____ *because He wants you to experience the best life possible*

Read Deuteronomy 7:7–8. This passage reveals the reason God loves us—he wants to love us. He promised his love to Israel's ancestors and God can never be accused of going back on his promises. The picture is one of God being tethered or attached to his people.

Hosea understood commitment. Some prophets used object lessons; Hosea became an object lesson. He was told to take as his wife a woman of questionable character—a harlot. This relationship symbolized Israel's relationship with God. The nation had been "married" to God but cheated on him by pursuing other gods.

> *In what ways are you "cheating" on your commitment to God?*

In the story, Hosea represents God. Hosea loved his wife as if she had been totally faithful to him. Likewise, God loves us as if we had maintained our faithfulness to him. But we all have moments of unfaithfulness. We stretch the truth, ignore our responsibilities, lose our tempers, and more. We can't go through the day without doing something that disappoints God. In spite of our unfaithfulness, God loves us in the same way Hosea loved his wife. The rest of the story is also symbolic. Hosea's wife was taken into slavery and Hosea was forced to pay a huge price to reclaim her.

> *What has taken people captive and what price has God paid to redeem us?*

REFLECT

Read Hosea 3:1–5. God's love for his people is not without purpose. In this passage, God revealed that Israel would eventually return to him. But before returning to God, they would experience the consequences of their spiritual rebellion. Going through the valley often reminds us of our need for God.

> *Describe your most recent spiritual valley. Was your valley experience a direct result of a change in your spiritual life? If so, how did your spiritual life change before, during, and after this experience?*

God's love for his people—you and me—isn't based on his emotion; it is based on his decision. It isn't something he feels; it is something he does. When God looks at us, he sees his Son . . .

if we have accepted Jesus Christ as our Savior and given him the right to be our Lord. God loved the world in this way: He gave his Son as payment for our sins.

In what ways is God's love similar to or different from our love?

If this is the way in which God loves us, what should be our response to him?

Jesus was the personification of love. He left heaven for the dusty floor of a carpentry shop. He swept floors and endured the intense Middle Eastern sun. He grew thirsty and was even ridiculed in his hometown. He was pursued by the religious power brokers and betrayed by a friend. Maybe you can relate. You might have experienced some situations similar to those Jesus experienced. Jesus stayed true to his calling and his mission. His mission was to buy us back. He could have said we weren't worth the trouble. He could have considered his own needs as being more important than ours. But he stayed, he lived, he suffered, he died, and he rose again. Why? Love . . . God's kind of love . . . agape love . . . love that won't let go.

God's love is unlike anything you and I can explain or understand. The only decision we have is to reject it or accept it.

REACT

"God so loved the world." This is a simple statement that has incredible ramifications. Love is offered from heaven to us. We simply have to accept it or reject it. Accepting God's love comes with conditions; rejecting it comes with consequences. Both the conditions of accepting it and the consequences of rejecting it are predetermined . . . by God. We don't get to set the terms. This is where so many potential believers balk—they want a relationship with God on their terms, not his. However, a relationship with God on any terms other than his is no relationship at all.

Describe the time when you first felt God's offer of his love. What was the setting and what was your response?

Describe situations in which you have attempted to define the terms of your relationship with God. What were the consequences of this decision?

> *Read Ephesians 3:18–19. What does this passage say about the degree of God's love for you?*

Others might devalue you, but God values you greatly. Others might say you are worthless, but God says you are worth loving. Others might remind you of past mistakes, but God forgives and forgets. God obviously has a plan for you!

5

THE ONLY
ONE AND ONLY

SCRIPTURE FOCUS:
John 14:1–14

LESSON OBJECTIVE:
To discover God's reliability and to commit to living with a constant awareness of his presence in your daily life.

"Jesus answered, 'I am the way and the truth and the life. No one comes to the Father except through me.'"

(John 14:6).

REWIND

Jesus's conversation with Peter is one of the most famous in the Bible. Jesus had just completed predicting Peter's denial of him. Peter and the other disciples were confused. Jesus was talking about going somewhere they could not go. For almost three years, they had been everywhere with him. They had given up their livelihoods for the opportunity to accompany Jesus. Now it appeared that relationship was coming to an end. Jesus was moving on and leaving his followers to fend for themselves . . . or so they thought.

The nature of their relationship was about to change. In John 14:16–17, Jesus promised them the Holy Spirit—a promise his followers surely didn't understand. Maybe his followers operated from the belief that Jesus would establish an earthly kingdom and they would all get important positions in his government. After all, this was the common belief of the day. Maybe they didn't understand who he *really* was—a pervasive problem we still face today!

RETHINK

Life is full of uncertainties. Some people agree that the only things certain are death and taxes. Well, these two certainly make the list.

What are some of the certain things in your life?

Review your list of certainties and place a plus sign (+) next to the positive statements and a negative sign (-) next to the negative statements. Do you have more positive or negative certainties? What does this say about your outlook on life?

If you have more negative than positive certainties in life, you might be more pessimistic than optimistic. Some degree of pessimism is helpful—it keeps us from believing everything. However, it is hard for us to experience spiritual growth in a pessimistic frame of mind. The negatives seem to overwhelm us and we get off course.

We all have some "due north" by which we set our courses. This is the marker that points us in the right direction. Ideally, God is our "due north." But that isn't always the case.

What are some of the other things by which you determine your direction in life?
_____ *ambition*
_____ *possessions*
_____ *popularity*
_____ *appearance*
_____ *family and/or friends*
_____ *emotions*
_____ *career*
_____ *other:* _____

REFLECT

Read John 14:1–14. Why were the disciples troubled? Their lives were about to be radically changed by events they didn't understand. We've all been there, haven't we? Jesus's words were intended to help his followers see the big picture. In doing so, they would overlook their troubling situations.

What troubling situations are you facing right now? Consider the following areas of life.

Home:

Relationships:

Career:

Spiritual Life:

Jesus promised to go and prepare a place for those who follow him. Based on the context, we can deduce that Jesus is speaking about heaven. The most encouraging promise is that those who trust Jesus will get to spend eternity with him (v. 3). Does that make today's problems disappear? No! But it does help us keep them in perspective. In light of eternity and the promises it holds, today's challenges are tiny blips on the radar screen of life.

For some people, Jesus's statement in verse 6 is one of the most difficult truths to accept. Jesus said that there is no other way to God except through him. This eliminates any faith that isn't built on faith in Jesus Christ and the idea that you can be good enough to earn a place in heaven. Jesus is the only way to heaven.

> *Is your faith religion-based or relationship-based? Explain your response.*

Religion-based faith focuses on keeping the rules. This was the trend in the first century and, for many, is still the trend today. People sometimes go to church as if *not* going might bring about bad luck. Others attend church but seem bothered to be there. Some people pay their taxes with more joy than they give to God's work. Others are more focused on what they get than how they invest themselves in the ministry. Religion-based faith is compartmentalized; that is, faith is separated from other aspects of life. This is religion-based faith and it doesn't open the door to heaven.

Take a look at what Jesus said in verse 7. He was speaking to his followers—the people who should have gotten it, who should have understood. Yet, he said, "If you had known me . . . ." Like us, the disciples often were more focused on themselves than on Jesus. In doing so, they missed who he really was. Jesus revealed God, but those who were closest to him missed it.

What does it mean to have relationship-based faith? It means to discover Jesus by spending time with him. Philip told Jesus, "Well, show us God and we'll get it this time." Jesus questioned Peter, "Have I been with you so long, and yet you have not known me, Philip?"

Rewrite Jesus's question to Philip substituting your name.

"Have I been with you so long, and yet you have not known me, _____?"

What can you do to keep this question from being asked of you?

REACT

Read Isaiah 55:8. We are unable to comprehend the ways in which God works. This means that our disappointments might eventually be viewed as something beneficial. You might already have seen this in your life.

> *What is one thing that has happened to you that seemed bad but eventually revealed itself to be beneficial?*

When Christ declares, "your Father knows the things you have need of" (Matthew 6:8 NKJV), believe it. After all, "He was in the beginning with God" (John 1:2 NKJV).

Jesus claims to be not a *top* theologian, an *accomplished* theologian, or even the *supreme* Theologian, but rather the *only* Theologian. "No one really knows the Father except the Son." He does not say, "No one really knows the Father *like* the Son" or "*in the fashion* of the Son." But rather, "No one really knows the Father except the Son."

Heaven's door has one key, and Jesus holds it.

6

THE HEART HE OFFERS

SCRIPTURE FOCUS:
2 Corinthians 5:16–21

LESSON OBJECTIVE:
To discover the life change that comes from an authentic relationship with God and commit to daily living within the boundaries of
that relationship.

"Therefore, if anyone is in Christ,
he is a new creation;
the old has gone, the new has come!"
(2 Corinthians 5:17).

REWIND

In the Bible, the heart is the center of human activity and emotion. The heart is the source of everything good and bad. The positive qualities of love and compassion are products of the heart. However, depravity and evil also are rooted there. Eventually, the concept of the heart grew to represent the entire person. Therefore, when the Bible speaks of renewing one's heart, the idea is that the entire person is to be renewed.

So, what changes when someone enters into a faith relationship with Jesus Christ? Some people change their habits. They habitually attend church a couple of times a week and might even pray on occasion. Some people change their priorities and pursue God's plans before their own desires. Other people change, period. This is the kind of change that represents the acquisition of a new heart.

RETHINK

"For from within, out of men's hearts, come evil thoughts, sexual immorality, theft, murder, adultery, greed, malice, deceit, lewdness, envy, slander, arrogance and folly" (Mark 7:21–22). Jesus understands why people are so messed up. It is a heart problem. Look at the problems Jesus connected to the heart.

On a scale of 1 to 5, with 1 being low and 5 being high, rate the degree to which each of the following are problems for you.
____ evil thoughts
__1__ sexual immorality

_____ *theft (stealing tangible or intellectual property)*
_____ *murder (which includes character assassination)*
_____ *adultery (which also includes lust)*
_____ *greed*
_____ *malice (depravity)*
_____ *deceit (deceptive dealings)*
_____ *lewdness (carousing)*
_____ *envy*
_____ *slander*
_____ *arrogance (pride)*
_____ *folly (foolishness)*

Based on your ratings, do you have a heart problem?
_____ *yes* _____ *no*

We all have some degree of a heart problem. We think evil thoughts without realizing we're thinking them. We can go down the list above and identify more problems, if we like. The issue isn't how bad we've been, but how fixed we can be.

How often do you recognize the influence of the Holy Spirit in your thought life?
_____ *never*
_____ *seldom*
_____ *sometimes*
_____ *often*
_____ *all the time*

> *What can you do to increase your awareness of the Holy Spirit in every area of your life?*

- Prayer and Fasting.
- Reading and obeying the Word of God.
- Come to church to worship.
- Be around spiritually mature people.

REFLECT

Read 2 Corinthians 5:16–21. We normally evaluate people against a human standard. We grade intelligence, appearance, and success as better than or worse than another person. In verse 16, Paul suggested that being in a relationship with Jesus Christ changes the criteria by which we evaluate people. The new criteria is Jesus Christ.

> *This changes everything. Take a look at verse 17. If anyone is in Christ, he or she is a new _____ _____ _____ _____ _____ _____ _____ _____.*
>
> *Therefore, if you are still thinking the thoughts and doing the things you did before you met Christ, you can conclude that you really aren't "in Christ." So, based on your thoughts and actions, are you in Christ or not? Explain your response.*

We inadvertently get it wrong when we say that we invited Jesus Christ into our lives. This suggests that he took up residence in the areas we assigned him. Maybe we allotted him Sundays, and we give him fifteen minutes to fix any problem we can't handle. This isn't real salvation! We don't invite Jesus into our lives; he invites us into his purpose. When we understand this nuance, we are ready to experience the life-changing power of God.

When we enter into a faith relationship with Jesus, we must leave behind things that are contrary to his nature. Verse 18 says that "now all things are of God." This is a great time to reflect on the significance of this statement as it relates to your life.

In your life, are all things of God? ____ *yes* ____ *no*

If so, what advice can you give someone who is struggling?
If not, what areas of life are you still controlling?

Romans 3:23 says that we are incapable of living the life God intended us to live. That might seem like bad news, but it sets the stage for a remarkable truth—God can live that life through us, if we allow him to inhabit every area of life. Rather than proclaim our self-confidence, we should humbly express our need for God. Only when we totally surrender to God will we be prepared to experience life the way God wants it to be—full, abundant, rewarding.

What is your heart condition? Place an X on the continuum below representing the state of your heart.

Hard-hearted————Lukewarm————Pure-hearted

The hard-hearted will never see God (Hebrews 12:14). The lukewarm make God sick to his stomach (Revelation 3:16). The pure-hearted will see God (Matthew 5:8). Jesus Christ offers a new heart—his heart. There is no preexisting condition that disqualifies you from the heart transplant. There is no co-pay or advance authorization required. You don't need insurance or time off work. You simply need to accept the offer.

REACT

Read 2 Corinthians 5:21. The heart transplant includes a complete overhaul at no extra charge. Jesus Christ took our sin on himself so that we can stand before God without fear of being banished to hell. But salvation is more than insurance against hell; it is the only way to experience life at its best.

The "good life" means different things to different people. What does it mean to you?

> *How has your concept of the "good life" been affected by*
> *your relationship with Jesus Christ?*
> *_____ I'm trying to convince Jesus that my way is best.*
> *_____ My faith and my life are not connected.*
> *_____ Jesus is in charge of parts of my life.*
> *_____ My concept of the "good life" has been totally*
> *revamped.*

Are you living life with a new heart? Are you seeing things from a godly perspective? If so, you can testify about God's power to change a person's life. If not, you have yet to accept Jesus's invitation to live in his purpose; you are not yet "in Christ." This isn't a game show where you can hope you're right; this is the difference between life with Christ or life without Christ. It's a decision that has present and eternal implications.

"For God made Christ, who never sinned, to be the offering for our sin, so that we could be made right with God through Christ."

7

HEAVEN'S "WHOEVER" POLICY

SCRIPTURE FOCUS:
Luke 16:19–31

LESSON OBJECTIVE:
To discover that no one is excluded from God's offer of salvation
and to commit to extending the offer to everyone we encounter.

*"Whoever is thirsty, let him come; and
whoever wishes, let him take the
free gift of the water of life"*
(Revelation 22:17).

REWIND

Religious elitism has plagued our world for centuries. Some people once believed they had an inside track on God. Today, that belief is alive and well. Some religions claim to have figured it out. Some denominations spend more time dissecting the beliefs of other denominations than understanding their own beliefs. But the Bible teaches something much different.

Whoever in the Bible is an all-inclusive term. In other words, no one is left out. The worst sinner, the vilest criminal, the most deceitful executive, and the most hard-hearted parent all are included in the *whoever* statement. You also are included in the *whoever* statements. When you read the Bible, you can substitute your name for any instance of *whoever*.

The story goes that a church was debating the amenities that were to be included in its new multi-purpose facility. After a long discussion, the decision was made to eliminate some recreational equipment because the church leaders didn't want the facility to become a hangout for the less-desirable people in the community. This church obviously didn't take the *whoever* statements in the Bible into consideration.

RETHINK

Some people believe that they are undesirable to God. Why? They obviously recognize God's holiness and their personal depravity. They see the gulf that separates them from God and see no way to cross from one side to the other.

> *Do you think that God desires a relationship with you?*
> *Why or why not?*

It is easy to recognize our need for God, but difficult to comprehend God's desire for a relationship with us. We can't add anything to God. As a matter of fact, we're probably more trouble than we're worth. So why does God desire to have a relationship with us and why would he allow his Son to be sacrificed so that the relationship could be made possible? It's because of his love for his creation.

REFLECT

Read Luke 16:19–31. Jesus told the parable of Lazarus and the rich man to prove a point. He wanted to redefine the terms of admission to heaven. People thought that heaven could be earned. In the story, Jesus tells the story of two men who died. One was rich, the other poor. After his death, the rich man was tormented in Hades. The poor man was in heaven at Abraham's side. Where the rich man had spent his life accumulating wealth, the poor man had spiritual treasures.

> *Which man are you most like?*
> _____ *The rich man trusting wealth and power.*
> _____ *The poor man trusting God's grace.*

Once in Hades, the rich man begged for someone to go back and warn his family members to do whatever was necessary to prevent spending eternity in hell. The problem was that the "whoever" policy has a statute of limitations—it must be invoked while the person is alive.

Your circle of influence is made up of people who are in need of a personal relationship with Jesus Christ. In the space provided below, list people in each category who need to be made aware of the whoever policy.

Family:

Friends:

Coworkers:

Neighbors:

Acquaintances:

Why have you not yet discussed spiritual matters with these people?

The rich man got some bad news from Abraham—after death, the gulf between the saved and the unsaved cannot be crossed. That was all the motivation the rich man needed. He begged that someone from death return to life to persuade his family members to repent and accept God's grace.

What obstacles did you overcome in order to accept God's offer of salvation?

What makes it difficult for people to accept the simplicity of Jesus's atonement?

Abraham told the man that people who do not believe in Moses and the Prophets wouldn't believe it if someone rose from the dead. For Jesus to tell this story was prophetic in and of itself. Jesus would indeed rise from the dead and people would continue to scoff. Today, there still are scoffers who don't believe what Scripture says and can't buy into the idea that Jesus really did rise from the dead.

REACT

God's *whoever* policy includes you and me and everyone else on the planet. As Christ-followers, it is our responsibility to (a) point people to God's love and, (b) not stand in the way of them seeing his love.

Is it easier for you to point people to God's love or to control your actions and attitudes so that you don't become a stumbling block to others? Explain your response.

Read Matthew 18:6–7. Sin is anything that separates a person from God. What is Jesus's attitude toward those who cause others to be separated from God?

_____ *It's not a big deal.*

_____ *It's deserving of a slap on the wrist.*

_____ *It's deserving of death.*

What are some things you do that misrepresent God to the world?

The very reason many people fail to accept God's offer of salvation is because of their encounters with people who claim to be believers. Maybe you've heard people say, "I'd probably be a Christian today if I didn't know so many people who claim to be Christians."

You might not think about your effect on a doubting world. How do you respond when you experience customer service that is far below your expectations? What do you say when the restaurant employee can't seem to get your order right? How do you deal with people who disappoint you? When you are driving, are you courteous and considerate or reckless and rude? (You might want to consider your driving habits before placing the fish on the rear of your vehicle!) When people encounter you, are they encouraged or disgusted? Are you a good advertisement for God's "whoever" policy?

8

BELIEVE AND RECEIVE

SCRIPTURE FOCUS:
1 John 1:1–10

LESSON OBJECTIVE:
To discover the true meaning of faith and to commit
to living in a faith-based relationship with God.

"If we confess our sins, he is faithful
and just and will forgive us our sins
and purify us from all unrighteousness."
(1 John 1:9).

REWIND

Belief. It's a word that we use with ease but exercise with caution. The mental decision to accept a statement as true or false bears fruit in your behavior. You can say that you believe the boat will safely transport you from one shore to the other, but your belief is merely speculation until you actually step foot on the boat. Believing and receiving are cause and effect statements.

We believe our sports teams will have great seasons. We believe our jobs are secure. We believe that this year will be better than last year. Sometimes the things we believe are little more than hopes based on wishful thinking. There is a line between wishes and beliefs. Wishes are based on desires; beliefs are based on facts. Is your place in heaven something you hope for or something you know to be a fact?

RETHINK

Why do we trust some people or situations and refuse to trust others? Trust is based on the perception of truth. We can't place our trust in something we believe to be untrue. Think about all of the advertising that causes you to question the truthfulness of the claims being made. Is that product really better than the other product? Is the endorser being paid to say the product is good or is his statement an unbiased personal belief? These questions about the claims that are made drive us to believe or not to believe what someone says.

In order to believe something, how much proof do you require?

What are some things you know to be true?

Do you have tangible proof for everything on the list above? If not, how is it possible to believe something you can't prove?

REFLECT

Read 1 John 1:1–10. John's letter wasn't based on wishful thinking; it was based on his personal experiences with Jesus. This was John the disciple—the same John who wrote the Gospel of John and was one of the closest companions of Jesus Christ.

Modern history books tell us stories of people we've never met and can't prove ever existed. Our money memorializes individuals we accept based on the testimony of generations. Few doubt the leadership of George Washington, the wisdom of Benjamin Franklin, or the courage of Abraham Lincoln. Yet no one who is alive today ever encountered one of those men. We simply accept their existence because history tells us they lived and we can see the effects of their accomplishments in our world today.

So, why don't people believe Jesus existed when the biblical and extra-biblical testimonies offer the same proof as that of the historical figures from our nation's history? The sad fact is that they don't want to believe. A college professor teaching an Old Testament class stated that he would choose to accept the Bible as fact until someone could prove it to be untrue. One of his students approached him later and said that his faith had been transformed by the professor's statement. If you want to believe in Jesus, there is ample evidence to support your belief. However, if you want to ignore Jesus, you can certainly find articulate arguments to support your lack of faith. It comes down to a question of your desire.

> *Do you really want to believe Jesus is who he claims to be? Why or why not?*

Reread 1 John 1:1. John's belief in Jesus was based on his personal experience with him. John heard, saw, and touched Jesus. John saw the things Jesus did. John could not deny Jesus's deity.

What are some things you have seen Jesus do in your life?

In what ways are those experiences affecting your willingness to talk about your faith?

In 1 John 1:6, John draws a line in the sand. The claim of discipleship must be supported in action. That must have been a problem in the first century; it still is a problem today. Walking in darkness can be explained as not "living what we claim" (MSG). What does this mean in everyday life? It means not making spending time with God a priority. It means greedily holding on to what rightfully belongs to God. It means seeking our own pleasure rather than seeking to serve God. It means living for our own purposes rather than for God's purposes.

If living what you claim is the test of authentic faith, how authentic is your faith?
_____ *My faith is the real deal.*
_____ *My faith is a thin veneer over a self-centered life.*

REACT

If you hang out around a car lot, you don't become a car. Likewise, if you hang out around believers, you don't become a believer. Becoming a believer is an act of your will. You become a believer when you take Jesus at his word, accept his control over your life, and act in obedience to his instructions.

Which of the following three steps have you completed?
_____ *I have taken Jesus at his word.*
_____ *I have accepted his control of my life.*
_____ *I am acting in obedience to his instructions.*

Which of the above is easiest? Which is hardest? Explain your responses.

In 1 John 1:9, we see the formula for a right relationship with God. Confess your sins. Confession is agreeing with God about your thoughts and actions. We can confess only when we stop making excuses for what we do. We must see our lives from God's perspective. Once we see our lives from his perspective, we will be broken and disappointed in ourselves. We then will seek God's forgiveness and he will forgive us. Read the end of 1 John 1:9 again. The verse says that he will "purify us from all unrighteousness." Then, and only then, will we be ready to have the quality of life that God intended.

Are you living proof of God's love and forgiveness or are you trapped in your sin because you want things done your way? Real belief requires change. So, when it comes to you and God, which one is required to change?

9

GOD'S GRACIOUS GRIP

SCRIPTURE FOCUS:
John 10:22–30

LESSON OBJECTIVE:
To discover the permanence of salvation and to commit to living
with confidence in God's power to keep us in his grip.

*"I give them eternal life, and
they shall never perish; no one
can snatch them out of my hand"*
(John 10:28).

REWIND

Getting a permanent (a.k.a. "perm") done on your hair might be one of the strangest concepts ever—after all, if it's "permanent," why does it have to be redone every three to six months? Shouldn't the permanent be renamed the "temporary"? This temporary nature of permanence applies to more than hair. Some people apply it to their spiritual lives, believing that God certainly can't follow through on the promise of once saved, always saved.

The Bible, however, teaches that salvation is indeed permanent, or else Jesus's words recorded in John 10 are little more than a smokescreen. If Jesus was incapable of telling a lie, then we must accept the fact that salvation is a "once and done" experience. We are saved one time, but the journey to spiritual maturity is a lifelong experience.

RETHINK

Jesus said that eternal life is something he gives; it isn't earned or deserved. Jesus did for us what we are incapable of doing for ourselves. The legalistic faith of first-century Judaism was cumbersome and confusing. They spent more time counting the steps someone took on the Sabbath than they did counting the costs of discipleship. The self-help theology of your local bookstore is equally cumbersome and confusing. One book might tell you that your problem is your diet. Another says the problem is exercise. Yet another says that success and security are a matter of positive thinking.

Throw into the mix the simple concept of salvation as a function of God's grace and some people get really confused. Solutions

to major problems usually require a summit or at least a commit-
tee, don't they?

How permanent is your salvation?
_____ *It can evaporate at any moment.*
_____ *It can survive if I do right.*
_____ *It is eternally secure.*

*How does your response to the question above affect your
spiritual life every day?*

REFLECT

Read John 10:22–30. We live in a culture where nothing is permanent. Everything we believe to be permanent is really hanging
by a thread, so it seems. It's easy to see how people might apply
worldly reasoning to spiritual situations. The fragile nature of
relationships makes it hard for us to believe that God's love is
eternal. The tenuous nature of our jobs makes it hard to believe
that God won't discard us in the same way our employers do.
We're a culture convinced that nothing is permanent.

Read John 10:28–29. What does this passage say to those who believe salvation can be lost just as easily as it was found?

What do you think makes people believe they can lose their salvation?

The key is this—salvation's permanence isn't based on my ability to keep it, but on God's ability to sustain it. When I doubt my salvation, I am expressing doubt about God's ability and desire to preserve our relationship. I am, in effect, saying that my ability to escape God is greater than his ability to hold on to me. That makes me more powerful than God. And that makes God a liar.

This doesn't mean we won't have spiritual highs and lows. Some days are better than others. There are times when we turn to God, express our deepest needs, and hear nothing. There are times when God delivers what we need long before we ever realized we needed it. God's activity is based on his timing, not ours. That can be frustrating.

What are three things you are praying about right now? How long have you been praying for each thing? What do you expect God's response to be?

Prayer isn't our opportunity to convince God to do things our way; it is our opportunity to align our lives with God's purposes. Sometimes the spiritual lows we experience are a direct result of praying for things that are not a part of God's plan. As long as we expect God to conform to our needs, our prayer life will have minimal effectiveness. When God doesn't respond the way we expect, we often doubt our relationship with him.

Think back on the past thirty days. What is one spiritual high point you have experienced? What is one spiritual low point you have experienced?

Did the spiritual high point have any effect on the permanence of your salvation? Did the spiritual low point mean that you were less saved than you were in the spiritual high point?

Jesus pointed out the problem. Take a look at verse 26. There is only one reason that you would ever doubt God's ability to preserve your salvation—you aren't one of his sheep. In other words, you might think you were saved, but you never really placed your trust in him. It's one thing to acknowledge Jesus's existence; it's another thing to put your faith in him.

REACT

We have faith in a lot of things—yet many of the things we trust are little more than temporary. You might not understand aerodynamics, but you don't hesitate to board an airplane. Why? Because of the track record. You trust because you are aware of the reliability of air travel in our country.

What have you seen God do in the lives of other people?

What have you seen God do in your own life?

Are you more trusting of the airline industry or of God? Explain your response.

Read Colossians 2:6–10. Receiving and believing are companion concepts. When writing to the Colossians, Paul referred to believing as "walking." The idea is that faith spills over into action. Action reaffirms faith. Reaffirmed faith spills over into action. This is the idea expressed as being "established in the faith." It is the same as being rooted or firmly planted. Your daily walk reveals the strength of your spiritual foundation.

If a casual observer followed you around for a day, would your actions reveal a dynamic, growing faith in God or would that person be convinced that God lacks the power to hold on to your life?

10

HELL'S SUPREME SURPRISE

SCRIPTURE FOCUS:
Matthew 7:13–23

LESSON OBJECTIVE:
To discover the seriousness of hell and to commit to living with
the desire to warn as many as possible of hell's ugliness.

*"Then I will tell them plainly, 'I never
knew you. Away from me, you evildoers!'"*
(Matthew 7:23).

REWIND

People joke about it. Some ignore it. There are even some who believe it couldn't possibly exist. What is it? A successful celebrity marriage? An unbiased journalist? A scandal-free political season? These all are good guesses, but they all are wrong. The correct response is hell. We sometimes think about it when we see devil costumes in the seasonal aisle at the local mega-market, but even then, we make it into something funny.

Why do we attempt to minimize hell? Well, for starters, if we acknowledge its existence, we have to acknowledge the criteria for admission. When we do that, we might discover that we have met the criteria for admission to hell, not heaven. It's one of those things we'd rather not talk about.

RETHINK

For some people, salvation is little more than fire insurance—they don't care about this life, they just don't want to burn in hell. Some people say they'd rather go to hell because that's where all of their friends will be. Well, let's clarify one thing—hell is not the place for companionship. Hell is experienced alone, not in community. It is eternal separation from God and everyone else. It is eternal punishment by way of fire. There will be no rest from the constant torment. Nothing about it sounds fun!

What is your first thought when you hear "hell"?

If you knew someone was in danger of spending eternity in hell, what would you do?
_____ *Stand by and do nothing.*
_____ *Hope for a future opportunity to discuss it.*
_____ *Try to get someone else to talk about it with the person.*
_____ *Do whatever is necessary to talk with the person now.*

If you are in danger of spending eternity in hell, what should you do?
_____ *Wait until later—when I'm old and done having fun.*
_____ *Hope that I'll get a waiver for being a good person.*
_____ *I'll get into heaven because I was raised in a Christian home.*
_____ *I should settle the issue right now because there are no guarantees in life.*

REFLECT

Read Matthew 7:13–23. Entering the city through the narrow gate meant leaving outside a person's possessions. It is interesting that Jesus compared salvation to entering through the narrow gate. Imagine yourself walking up to the gate: In your backpack you have all of the good things you've done and all of your possessions. You have souvenirs of your accomplishments and trophies from your conquests. Yet, the gate won't allow you and the baggage to pass through. You either stand outside with your baggage or you leave your baggage and enter alone. Once you get inside, you realize that everything you thought was valuable is behind and you are left to stand on your own. What you accumulated and accomplished is insignificant; all you have is your relationship with Christ.

What are you counting on to give you access to heaven?

Will the things you are currently valuing make it easier or harder for you to live a life of faith?

Heaven and hell are real. Your choices in this life have eternal significance. You can desire heaven, but apart from a relationship with God, it will never be realized. A relationship with God requires you to agree with God about your sin and to submit yourself to his guidance. From now on, you must make important those things that God says are important and unimportant those things God says are unimportant.

Consider your daily activities. What are your top five priorities? Be honest.

1.

2.

3.

4.

5.

Now consider your life from God's perspective. What should be your top five priorities?

1.

2.

3.

4.

5.

Explain any mismatches.

Whenever we make important things that God says are unimportant, we are living in disobedience to God. In other words, we are holding onto the backpack while trying to squeeze through the narrow gate. We're stuck until we let go.

What are some things you need to release in order to be in a right relationship with God?

What is keeping you from releasing these things?

False spirituality is no spirituality at all. Read Matthew 7:15–20. Real faith is revealed in changed lives. When we are living to please God, we do the things that matter to him. We say the godly things and think the godly thoughts. Jesus warned people to distance themselves from faith that doesn't call for and produce life change.

In what ways is your faith affecting your daily life?

How different are you from people who do not know God?
____ *I'm just like them . . . a "secret service" Christian.*
____ *I don't think the thoughts and do the things I used to do.*

There is a danger in falling for easy faith. Read Matthew 7:21–23. Can these words be said of you? Why or why not?

REACT

Hell is real. It is not a party. You won't see your friends. It is a place of agony reserved for those who refuse to accept God's permanent offer of eternal life. In John 3:16, the idea "perish" is equated to eternal punishment. Those are the two choices: eternity in heaven or eternity in hell.

What is your choice—heaven or hell?

How do you know your relationship with God is real?

When it comes to facing death, will you face it with joy or with dread? Your answer says a lot about your spiritual condition. There is a lot of life to live and we should live it with passion and purpose. Yet, when this life comes to an end, we will be ushered into eternity based on the choice we made while we were alive. You can have peace today and hope for eternity. The choice is yours.

11

WHAT MAKES HEAVEN HEAVENLY

SCRIPTURE FOCUS:
Revelation 21:1–26

LESSON OBJECTIVE:
To discover the awesomeness of heaven and
to commit to living in this life as a resident of heaven.

"He will wipe every tear from their eyes.
There will be no more death or
mourning or crying or pain, for
the old order of things has passed away"
(Revelation 21:4).

REWIND

Heaven. The mention of the word probably brings many images to mind. Some of these images might be more influenced by culture than by Scripture. For you, heaven might be a replica of something you have experienced on earth. It might be more reminiscent of a high-priced luxury vacation than an eternal destination.

Maybe you don't think about heaven very much. This life might have more than enough busyness to keep your mind occupied. Yet the reality of an eternity in heaven can provide endless peace in times of despair and difficulty. Heaven won't be you wearing a white robe, sitting on a cloud strumming a golden harp, singing old songs from the hymnal. As a matter of fact, heaven isn't about you! It's about God and our spending eternity in his presence.

RETHINK

Have you ever thought about living in a perfect world? Think about what that would mean—no need to lock your doors because there would be no crime. The weather would be perfect. Everyone would be honest and at peace. No wars. No problems. No pain.

If you could live in a perfect world, would you? Why or why not?

The truth is that you and I *can* live in a perfect world. Maybe we can't live there now, but the time is coming when it will be possible. No matter how bad life gets, we can look forward to spending eternity in a perfect place. This is where life began—a place that was perfect. Adam and Eve lived there until they were evicted. Since then, humanity has looked forward to the day when that perfection might be experienced again.

> *If someone asked you to describe heaven, what would you say?*

The biblical writers tried to put into human words a description of a place that was beyond words. In the same way that it is impossible to describe God, it is impossible to describe heaven. We don't know what it is like to live in a perfect place. But you have the option of being there. The other choice is a place we don't want to describe—hell. In this case, making no choice is choosing hell.

REFLECT

Read Revelation 21:1–26. John was given an opportunity to see things that no person had ever seen before. The entire book of Revelation presents a picture of end times and of life beyond our earthly existence. The descriptions are the best John could offer.

He saw the unbelievable and had to try to explain it to believers and non-believers alike.

> *Why does God want us to spend eternity with him in heaven?*
> ____ *He needs the company.*
> ____ *He needs the entertainment.*
> ____ *He wants us to be bored.*
> ____ *He loves us.*

In Revelation 21, John begins by pointing out that the "first earth had passed away." Staying on this planet with things the way they are isn't an option. Like it or not, you will get to relocate for eternity. What John saw was something new—a new city in which God and man will live together in peace. All of the pains of life will disappear.

Those who failed to choose to spend eternity in heaven with God choose, by default, to be cast into the eternal lake of fire. But choosing heaven is much more than getting a free pass; it is allowing God to live in and through us until the time at which he calls us home. It's the abundant life now and the unbelievable life later.

> *What are some of the problems with which you deal on a regular basis?*

How would it be to have those problems disappear forever?

That's what heaven will be. God promised that the tears would be wiped away and that death would be eliminated. In verse 22, John reports that there was no temple in heaven.

Why will there not be a place of worship in heaven?

Heaven, by definition, will be a place of worship. That's what worship is—the natural response to being in God's presence. Because we will be in God's presence all the time, we will be worshiping all the time. There will be no interpersonal problems, no deceit, no overcrowded schedules. We will live in the light of God's presence and will offer our praise to him all the time.

Does this sound like a place you would like to be? Why or why not?

REACT

Go back and read Genesis 1. In the beginning, God designed a place where everything was good. Since that time, we have redefined *good*. We have equated *good* with castles, cars, and careers. We have lowered the standard so that we can experience things we believe to be good. But good isn't good unless it's of God.

What parts of your life are good?

What could make those things better?

When the things we define as good could be made better, we have missed God's concept of good. For God, *good* was the supreme expression of his creation. Good had no better. When God declared creation to be good, it wasn't good enough or a temporary state until something better could be done. Good was perfect and that's what heaven is.

Do you want to spend eternity in the place God calls *good*? If so, confess your sins and ask God to forgive you. Then commit your life to serving and pleasing God. As you live, you will discover how great it is to be in God's presence doing his work. This is abundant life. Why don't you join?

12

THE LAST WORD ON LIFE

SCRIPTURE FOCUS:
1 Peter 1:3–12

LESSON OBJECTIVE:
To discover the hope that God provides
and to commit to living in light of his hope.

*"Praise be to the God and Father
of our Lord Jesus Christ! In his
great mercy he has given us new birth
into a living hope through the resurrection
of Jesus Christ from the dead"*

(1 Peter 1:3).

REWIND

We all live with hope. We hope it will be a pretty day. We hope our kids behave. We hope the traffic isn't bad. We hope there is no bad news today. But what is hope? In the Bible, hope is more than wishful thinking—it is calm assurance. When the Bible mentions the "hope of heaven," it isn't talking about our hoping we get into heaven, but the hope that comes from the reality of heaven.

A young man was traveling from the United States to Canada shortly after the law was changed to require a passport to make the trip by air. With urgent processing and overnight delivery, the passport still didn't make it in time. The trip could not be canceled. This wasn't pleasure; it was business. So he left on the trip with the hope that he would be allowed to enter Canada and return to the United States. On the day of his return, he called home and told his parents that he had cleared all of the checkpoints; he would soon be on his way home.

At what point do you think the young man experienced real hope? It was when he had cleared the checkpoint and all doubts were erased. Before that, he didn't have hope; he only had wishful thinking.

RETHINK

Do you live with the calm assurance that God will do what he says he will do? Maybe you've been let down more times than you can count. You've been hurt in relationships and business. Everyone you ever thought was reliable has proven to be unreliable. That's the way it seems sometimes.

What are the things and/or people you know you can count on?

Why are you so sure?

At a time when today's solution is tomorrow's scandal, people are searching for something to believe. They want to believe that they will be secure, but realize that security is situational. They want to be happy, but happiness seems circumstantial. They want to be independent, but realize that they can't really trust themselves. Self-help books are flying off the shelves as people look for solutions.

Read 1 Peter 1:3–5. What is the assurance you find in these verses?

REFLECT

Why did God make it possible for us to spend eternity in heaven? It wasn't because of our goodness, but because of his mercy. Today we can have hope.

> *Read 1 Peter 1:3. What kind of hope do we have? What does this mean to us?*

"Living hope" means that it isn't something we store away for the future; it is alive. The hope we have empowers us to live today the way God intended it to be lived. What we hope for won't fade or shrink in significance because it is "incorruptible and undefiled."

Peter went on to explain that our faith is secured not by us, but by God. When we experience salvation, we are permanently assigned a place in heaven. No one can take it away. We can't be denied access later in life.

> *What does the assurance of eternity in heaven mean to you? How does it affect your daily life?*

This doesn't mean that life is easy. Peter acknowledged life's trials but assured his readers that the opportunity to spend eternity in heaven with God is worth the earthly struggle. Have you ever camped out all night to be one of the first to purchase the latest game system or tickets to the big game? Have you ever stood in the rain so that you might get the chance to be directly in front of the stage when your favorite musician performed?

> Why are we willing to tolerate such inconvenience in order to do the things listed above?
>
> In what ways is eternity in heaven better than the things listed above?

We get so turned around. We make important the things that are temporary and minimize the permanent things in life. We go to a lot of trouble to do things that will please us for a moment but ignore that thing that will provide peace for today and hope for the future. We live for the present, not for eternity.

REACT

Jesus has been to Bethlehem, wearing barn rags and hearing sheep crunch their hay. Suckling milk and shivering against the cold. All of divinity content to cocoon itself in an eight-pound body and to sleep on a cow's supper. Millions who face the chill of empty pockets or the fears of sudden change turn to Christ. Why?

Because he's been there.

He's been to Nazareth, where he made deadlines and paid bills; to Galilee, where he recruited direct reports and separated fighters; to Jerusalem, where he stared down critics and stood up against cynics.

We have our Nazareths, as well—demands and due dates. Jesus wasn't the last to build a team; accusers didn't disappear with Jerusalem's temple. Why seek Jesus's help with your challenges? Because he's been there. To Nazareth, to Galilee, to Jerusalem.

But most of all, he's been to the grave. Not as a visitor, but as a corpse. Buried amidst the cadavers. Numbered among the dead. Heart silent and lungs vacant. Body wrapped and grave sealed. The cemetery. He's been buried there.

You haven't yet. But you will be. And since you will, don't you need someone who knows the way out?

LEADER'S
GUIDE

CHAPTER 1: THE MOST FAMOUS CONVERSATION IN THE BIBLE

Scripture Focus: John 3:1–12

Lesson Objective: To discover that real life can only be found in a faith relationship with Jesus Christ and to commit to living within that relationship.

Before the small group session read Chapter 1 of 3:16.

The Context: This is our first encounter with Nicodemus, a member of the Pharisees. The Pharisees were the most significant Jewish party in New Testament times. They are pictured as being in opposition to Jesus's ministry. In addition to Nicodemus, Paul also was a Pharisee. The Pharisees controlled the synagogues and exerted considerable influence over the entire culture. The term "Pharisee" means "separated one" and probably refers to the practice of being separated for the purpose of studying the law. For them, the way to God was through total obedience to the law. The concept of grace was outside their realm of possibility.

Getting Started: Enlist a volunteer to read aloud John 3:1–12. Take a few moments to establish the context for this passage.

Discovering the Truth: Play the video clip for Lesson 1. Direct members to respond to the first question in the *Rethink* section of the Study Guide. Discuss some of the things people have tried in order to make sense out of life.

1. I'M IMPRESSED (JOHN 3:1–2). Nicodemus admitted that the Pharisees had taken note of Jesus's actions and credited them to God. What had Jesus done up to this point? He was baptized in the Jordan River (Matthew 3:13) and then tempted by Satan in the wilderness (Matthew 4:1–11). He chose the first five disciples (John 1:38–51) and then went to Cana to the wedding ceremony where he changed the water to wine (John 2:6–10). From Cana, he traveled to Capernaum and then to Jerusalem for the Passover. There he cleansed the temple (John 2:14–16). Obviously, in the early days of his ministry, Jesus got the attention of the Jewish officials.

Discuss some of the things Jesus is doing that might cause people to be curious about him. What can we do to make sure that we give credit to Jesus rather than taking personal credit for the things he is doing?

2. THAT'S IMPOSSIBLE (JOHN 3:3–8). When questioned about his actions, Jesus was quick to explain to Nicodemus that understanding them required a spiritual transformation that had not yet taken place in Nicodemus. Jesus used the phrase "born again" to describe the transformation. Write the following three words on the board: *earned, deserved, given*. Call for class members to identify the word that best describes how a person obtains eternal life. Use the questions regarding being born again under the *Rethink* section to guide your discussion of this topic.

3. YOU DON'T UNDERSTAND (JOHN 3:9–12). It sounds contradictory, but Jesus identified Nicodemus's problem—he was too religious to understand matters of faith. This leads to what many have called the most important verse in Scripture. Play the video clip for lesson one. Write the following on the board:

He loves.
He gave.
We believe.
We live.

Why is it so hard for some people to accept this simple spiritual truth? List responses on the board.

Point out that there are two philosophies identified in John 3:13. Draw a vertical line on the board and on the left side write "God/eternal" and on the right side write "world/perish." The vertical line is a solid barrier that we cannot cross without help. Nothing on the right side of the line will lead us to God. We must accept God's help. Erase a small portion of the center line and write "Jesus" in the middle. This is the only way to move from the right to the left.

Making It Real: Read aloud John 19:38–42. Point out the change that Nicodemus experienced. Call for volunteers to describe the changes that have taken place in their lives since they accepted Jesus as their Lord and Savior. Discuss some of the situations in which we are tempted to hide our relationships with God and how God feels when that happens. It is one thing to have an academic knowledge of God; it is another thing to know him through experience. Ask: *When it comes to your faith, are you studying it or are you experiencing it?* Close with prayer.

CHAPTER 2: NO ONE LIKE HIM

Scripture Focus: Isaiah 40:18–31

Lesson Objective: To discover that God is in the midst of every detail of life—no matter how small—and to commit to trusting him in every situation.

Before the small group session read Chapter 2 of 3:16.

The Context: The Israelites were having issues with their faith. They were headed for exile in Babylon and felt as if God had forgotten them. The middle portion of Isaiah (chapters 40–55) shows us that the Israelites were in captivity as part of God's disciplinary hand, not because the gods of the Babylonians were more powerful than the God of Israel. This middle section of the book offers hope for the exiles' ultimate return to their homeland. It serves as a call to a renewed faith in and commitment to the Lord who had proven himself to them over and over.

Getting Started: Enlist a volunteer to read aloud Isaiah 40:18–31. Take a few moments to establish the context for this passage.

Discovering the Truth: Play the video clip for Lesson 2. Write on the board "Why me?" and "Why now?" Call for volunteers to briefly describe situations in which they have asked these questions. Direct members to respond to the first activity in the *Rethink* section of the Study Guide. Discuss some of the ways people respond when they begin experiencing the consequences of their disobedience.

1. INCOMPARABLE POWER (ISAIAH 40:18–20). The people of Israel had been on a spiritual roller coaster. There had been twists and turns, highs and lows, slow climbs and rapid descents. They toyed with the pagan worship of the Canaanites because it

was more appealing to their carnal instincts. In other words, they looked for or created a religion that allowed them to set the boundaries—much the way things are done today.

Isaiah called out the people for their wishy-washy faith and demanded that they find a god equal to Yahweh God.

Arrange the class in small groups or in pairs and instruct them to write a modern paraphrase of verses 18–20, substituting contemporary idols for those listed in the passage. Call for volunteers to read aloud their paraphrases.

2. UNDENIABLE EVIDENCE (ISAIAH 40:21–26). The Israelites were focused more on their circumstances than on the God of their circumstances. They had forgotten or ignored everything God had done on their behalf. Before we criticize them too quickly, we should stop to consider how we often are just like the Israelites; we often see God clearly when things are good, but lose sight of him when life gets tough. What evidence of God had the Israelites experienced? They had heard the stories of how God affected the lives of their ancestors—the crossing of the Red Sea, the taking of the Promised Land, the face-off with Goliath and the Philistines, the battles they won and the ways in which God provided for his people. They also had firsthand experience—many of them had seen God at work in their lives and the lives of fellow Israelites.

Discuss modern evidence of God's activity and how God's actions should affect the faith of those who claim to be his children.

3. UNFATHOMABLE LOVE (ISAIAH 40:27–31). The Israelites not only thought that they had been forgotten by God, but also that they were invisible to God. God had promised to make them a blessing to all nations, but they were in exile in Babylon. How would they bless the nations from this situation? The lesson is that

God is true to his promises on his terms and in his time. It was through Israel that Jesus was born to the world. We make a mistake of believing that God's blessings through his people are limited to our generation. The Israelites couldn't see the big picture.

In spite of their lack of faith, God loved the Israelites. In spite of our lack of faith, God loves us. In the midst of what the Israelites believed to be a storm, God spoke the familiar words of verse 31 (NKJV):

> But those who wait upon the Lord
> Shall renew their strength;
> They shall mount up with wings like eagles,
> They shall run and not be weary;
> They shall walk and not faint.

Waiting requires patience. While waiting, God's people are spiritually and physically renewed. Then, no matter what their level of activity, they will be energized because their strength comes from their relationships with God.

Discuss how God's people can grow in the midst of waiting for God. Identify some of the sources of spiritual growth that are available through your church.

It is easy to become so focused on our situations that we lose all sight of God's activity in and through our lives. We must constantly be reminded that God is bigger than the problems we face and the things that get us down. God loves us and wants us to have the kind of life he intended for us all along—the abundant life.

Making It Real: Remind the class that God cannot be described in human terms. Read aloud Psalm 113:4–6 and call for volunteers to suggest some adjectives that can be used to describe God. List responses on the board. Close the lesson with a season of prayer encouraging class members to use the adjectives on the board as the basis for their prayers.

CHAPTER 3: HOPE FOR THE HARD HEART

Scripture Focus: Exodus 32:1–35

Lesson Objective: To discover the sources of a hardened heart and commit to renewing a vibrant relationship with God.
Before the small group session, read Chapter 3 of 3:16.

The Context: Three months earlier, the Israelites were slaves to the Egyptian pharaoh. Then, God intervened and, through a series of plagues, pharaoh released the captive nation allowing them to seek out the land that had been promised to Abraham, Isaac, and Jacob—the Promised Land. Their joyful escape from Egypt was short-lived as pharaoh changed his mind and pursued the Israelites to the shore of the Red Sea. Miraculously, the Red Sea opened and the Israelites crossed on dry land before witnessing pharaoh and his army being swallowed up by the angry waters. After a brief celebration, the people journeyed southeast toward Mount Sinai where they set up camp. Along the way, they saw God provide guidance, food, and victory. No one doubted God's existence or his love for his people . . . until the memory of those events grew dim. With Moses in conversation with God, the people turned to Aaron, Moses's older brother, for spiritual guidance. The golden calf was crafted and the people of God reverted to pagan worship practices.

Getting Started: Enlist several volunteers to read aloud portions of Exodus 32:1–35. Take a few moments to establish the context for this passage.

Discovering the Truth: Write on the board "hardened heart." Call for volunteers to define "hardened heart" and to briefly describe situations that might cause one's heart to be hardened. Be prepared to define the term from the biblical perspective as resistance to or rejection of God's Word and/or his will. Direct members to respond to the first activity in the *Rethink* section of the Study Guide. Call for volunteers to share briefly about their experiences with hardened hearts.

1. SELFISH IMPATIENCE (EXODUS 32:1). God seldom does anything according to our schedules. That is true today and it was true when the Israelites were encamped at the base of Mount Sinai. Moses led them out of Egypt and now he was absent as he attended a meeting with God. In the meeting, God provided Moses instructions about almost every area of life. Meanwhile, down below, Aaron was fashioning a golden calf for the people to worship.

Discuss some of the reasons people grow impatient with God. List responses on the board. Make two columns on the board and write *positive* above the first column and *negative* above the second column. Call for volunteers to suggest some of the consequences of growing impatient with God. List responses in the appropriate column of the chart on the board.

2. MISDIRECTED WORSHIP (EXODUS 32:2–6). The Israelites had followed Moses for three months and witnessed God's intervention on their behalf on several occasions. Yet, with Moses on

the mountain, they returned to doing what they had done in Egypt—they crafted an idol to worship. The cow or bull was a common idol in Egyptian and Canaanite pagan religions. It is interesting, however, that Aaron associated the idol with the "feast to the Lord" (v. 5).

Discuss some ways that we incorporate worldliness into our worship of God. What "idols" do we inappropriately associate with God? What can be done to keep our worship of God pure?

3. RIGHTEOUS INDIGNATION (EXODUS 32:7–29). God wasn't happy with the behavior of the Israelites. He told Moses that they were a "stiff-necked people" (v. 9). Moses pleaded with God to spare his people. When Moses returned to the camp, he encountered the joyful worship of the idol and questioned Aaron about it. Aaron, who had crafted the idol, claimed that he cast the golden jewelry into the fire and the calf simply appeared.

Aaron wanted to blame God for his bad decision. In what ways do we do the same thing?

Even though God relented, the people still suffered destruction when Moses instructed those who were on the Lord's side to go throughout the camp killing those who were not on God's side. That day, three thousand people died (v. 28).

God did not bring about the destruction; he allowed it to happen. God relented from destroying the people himself, but he did not relent from allowing his judgment to fall. Moses called for repentance and recommitment to God. The lesson here is that repentance is always an option for those who fail God. The other option is judgment.

4. RENEWED PURPOSE (EXODUS 32:30–35). Moses returned to his audience with God and pleaded on behalf of the Israelites. He confessed their sin and asked God for forgiveness. God did

forgive those who repented, but those who did not were plagued from that day forward.

What are some things we can do to prevent experiencing God's wrath? Discuss some preventive measures for avoiding or dealing with temptation.

The same thing happens today. Many people sin against God, refuse to repent, and are plagued. They live in spiritual frustration searching for purpose and meaning in life. When we sin, the only way to rediscover our purpose in life is to confess our sin and seek God's forgiveness. Better yet, the choice would be to avoid the need to confess by seeking to do what God intended in the first place.

Making It Real: Play the video clip for Lesson 3. Discuss some of the things that cause people's hearts to harden. Remind the class that God pursues us even when we run from him. God pursues us even when we stick our noses where we shouldn't. God pursues us because "God so loved the world." As you lead the class in prayer, read this quote from *3:16:* "Is your heart hard? Take it to your Father. You're only a prayer away from tenderness. You live in a hard world, but you don't have to live with a hard heart."

CHAPTER 4: WHEN YOU GET BOOTED OUT

Scripture Focus: Hosea 3:1–5

Lesson Objective: To discover God's relentless love and commit to living in a right relationship with our heavenly Father.
Before the small group session read Chapter 4 of 3:16.

The Context: The Northern Kingdom—Israel—had been unfaithful to God. Ever since leaving Egypt, the people had struggled with their spiritual commitment. Sometimes they would boldly declare their allegiance to him but then quickly return to practicing elements of pagan worship. If the relationship between God and Israel was a marriage, Israel was the unfaithful partner.

As a prophet to Israel, Hosea saw the nation's final six kings. The text suggests that Hosea and Isaiah were contemporaries. The book of Hosea reveals a balanced picture of God—his love and his jealousy. Hosea's ministry was focused on challenging the increasingly popular practice of Baal worship. With the nation in political strife, the spiritual condition of the nation was in a tailspin. The Assyrian empire was expanding and eventually would control Israel and Judah.

Hosea and his wife, Gomer, had three children with symbolic names—Jezreel (a reminder of the nation's actions at Jezreel), LoRuhamah (meaning "not loved"), and Lo-Ammi (meaning "not my people"). Gomer was a wayward woman and eventually became the property of another man. Hosea was instructed to purchase her back, which he did. The picture was one of God's love for his people.

Getting Started: Enlist a volunteer to read aloud Hosea 3:1–5. Take a few moments to establish the context for this passage.

Discovering the Truth: Write on the board "Why does God want to have a relationship with you?" Call for volunteers to respond to the question. Direct members to respond to the first activity in the *Rethink* section of the Study Guide. Point out that God's love is always for the purpose of giving us the best possible life.

However, the "good life" that many people pursue has little to do with God's concept of the "good life" he wants to provide.

1. DO OVER (HOSEA 3:1). Hosea was unique because he was tuned in to God. Notice that this verse begins with "then" indicating that Hosea already had heard from God in the past. God's instruction to Hosea is to "start all over" (3:1 MSG). Gomer had moved out and was living with her latest boyfriend. She had become a slave to a lifestyle that was dishonoring to Hosea and to God. Yet God didn't order Hosea to discard her; he orders Hosea to get her back.

The comparison is made to the Israelites and their relationship with God. The Israelites were essentially sleeping with pagan gods. They had become spiritual free agents and used their religious practices for self-indulgence. In what ways are people today like the Israelites? Discuss how believers are tempted toward modern forms of idolatry.

2. DO BETTER (HOSEA 3:2–3). God would not allow his people to continue in their spiritual rebellion against him. He symbolically bought them back. Gomer's isolation from her family is symbolic of Israel's isolation in the Babylonian Exile. Though they would become the property of the Babylonians, the nation eventually would be returned to their homes. Though the people had strayed from God, they eventually would be in a right relationship with him once again.

Read aloud Deuteronomy 7:7–8 and discuss God's determination to love us. Point out that his love is rooted in his historical promise and his character. Discuss some of the ways people "cheat" on their relationships with God. Remind members that daily maintaining a strong relationship with God is their best defense against spiritual missteps.

3. DO ENDURE (HOSEA 3:4–5). Things were going to get worse before they got better. The Israelites would spend seventy years in Babylonian captivity before they were allowed to return home. Upon returning home, they would discover the things weren't the way they dreamed they would be. Many of the structures were in ruins and the land was inhabited by other people groups. The Israelites who remembered Israel's glory were gone and a new generation was left to start over.

This is where we see that God's love does not override his justice. The people had sinned and set in motion a series of events that would not be stopped. These events were the direct consequences of their rebellion. God's love was there, but he could not reward bad behavior.

The same is true in our lives—we make bad decisions and rebel against God. God loves us, will forgive us, but will not intervene in the consequences we invite into our lives. Call for volunteers to share their experiences with bad decisions and their consequences.

The promise to Israel was that they would eventually return to God and his ways. But, Israel had to forsake their idols and seek God on his terms. The same is true of us today. Discuss the terms of God's relationship with his people.

What does God expect or require? Read aloud Micah 6:8 pointing out the three things God demands—to act justly, to love mercy, and to walk in humble obedience to him.

Making It Real: Play the video clip for Lesson 4. Bring the class to a close by reading the following quote from *3:16*:

"I have a feeling that most people who defy and deny God do so more out of fear than conviction. For all our chest pumping and braggadocio, we are anxious folk—can't see a step into the future, can't hear the One who owns us. No wonder we try to gum the hand that feeds us.

"But God reaches and touches. He speaks through the immensity of the Russian plain and the density of the Amazon rain forest. Through a physician's touch in Africa, a bowl of rice in India. Through a Japanese bow or a South American *abraço*. He's even been known to touch people through messages like the ones you are [studying]. If he is touching you, let him.

"Mark it down: God loves you with an unearthly love."

Close with prayer.

CHAPTER 5: THE ONLY ONE AND ONLY

Scripture Focus: John 14:1–14

Lesson Objective: To discover God's reliability and to commit to living with a constant awareness of his presence in your daily life. *Before the small group session read Chapter 5 of 3:16.*

The Context: Nearing the end of his earthly ministry, Jesus shared some disturbing news with his disciples. He told them that he would be betrayed by Judas (John 13:21), that he would be leaving them (John 13:33), and that Peter would deny him (John 13:38). The disciples didn't believe what Jesus said because they didn't understand it.

Jesus took advantage of the opportunity to point out the differences between being acquainted with him and really knowing him.

Just because his disciples had spent time with him didn't mean they really knew him. The same is true today. Time spent in religious activities doesn't automatically translate into spiritual growth.

Getting Started: Enlist a volunteer to read aloud John 14:1–14. Take a few moments to establish the context for this passage.

Discovering the Truth: Play the video clip for Lesson 5. Call for volunteers to identify some of the things in life about which they are certain. List responses on the board. Review the list, marking positive certainties with a plus sign (+) and negative certainties with a minus sign (-). Call attention to the activity in which members are asked to identify some of the things by which they determine their direction in life. Discuss responses.

1. CALM ASSURANCE (JOHN 14:1–4). Jesus had just delivered disturbing news to the disciples—he was leaving them. What they needed was assurance, not an explanation. He offered assurance by telling them that he would prepare a place for them in heaven. The secret to peace in any situation is total trust in Jesus Christ. How can we trust God in the midst of trials? By remembering that our real home is heaven and that we will live for eternity in a place Jesus prepared especially for us.

Discuss the peace that the assurance of salvation provides. Recount situations in which the assurance of salvation has sustained you through a difficult or trying situation. Call for volunteers to share similar stories.

2. TROUBLING CONFUSION (JOHN 14:5–11). Three years as Jesus's closest friends wasn't enough to comfort Thomas, Philip, and the others. Thomas took Jesus's figurative language literally

and missed the point. Philip expected Jesus to pull back the curtains of heaven revealing God to the disciples. Both disciples were well intentioned, but confused.

Jesus questioned what the disciples had learned during their time with him. Philip was acquainted with Jesus but he did not have an intimate knowledge of him. Maybe they saw Jesus as a spiritually gifted man. But they couldn't see God. The same thing is true today; many people know about Jesus, but they don't really know him. They are fans, not followers. Discuss some ways to improve one's relationship with Jesus. List responses on the board. Point out that Jesus's goal was to teach the world what God is really like.

3. LIFE SIMPLIFIED (JOHN 14:12–14). Jesus never intended for our faith relationships with him to be complicated; he wanted us to have a simple faith. Life is simplified when our needs are in line with God's will. Jesus never offered to give us everything we want; he offered to answer prayers that are in line with his purposes. Once we are in right relationships with him, we will cease praying selfish prayers. We will focus on serving and pleasing him.

Discuss how believers determine between needs and wants. Point out how our spiritual lives will be improved when we pray for the things that matter to Jesus rather than those things that we want.

We must be careful not to pray selfishly or presumptuously. We can pray for people to be healed, but we must allow for the fact that it's not always God's will to heal all people. When we ask in Jesus's name, we are aligning our wills with his will; not manipulating God so that he does what we want.

Why are our spiritual lives in such disarray? It's usually because we are confused about who God is and what He is doing in our lives. We want to control every aspect of life and nod to God in appreciation for what happens.

Making It Real: Bring the class to a close by reading the following quote from *3:16:*

"But can we trust him? Only one way to know. Do what I did in Rio. Seek him out. Lift up your eyes, and set your sights on Jesus. No passing glances or occasional glimpses. Enroll in his school. 'Let me teach you . . .' Make him your polestar, your point of reference. Search the crowded streets and shadow-casting roofs until you spot his face, and then set your sights on him.

"You'll find more than a hospital.

"You'll find the Only One and Only."

Close with prayer.

CHAPTER 6: THE HEART HE OFFERS

Scripture Focus: 2 Corinthians 5:16–21

Lesson Objective: To discover the life change that comes from an authentic relationship with God and commit to daily living within the boundaries of that relationship.

Before the small group session read Chapter 6 of 3:16.

The Context: Reconciliation was one of the main themes of Paul's second letter to the Christians in Corinth. Though Paul took plenty of criticism, his defense usually centered around the person and power of Jesus Christ. The criticism Paul received from the false prophets in Corinth caused him to address a significant portion of the second letter to some foundational faith issues. In this passage, Paul discussed the importance of being reconciled to God.

Getting Started: Enlist a volunteer to read aloud 2 Corinthians 5:16–21. Take a few moments to establish the context for this passage.

Discovering the Truth: Enlist a volunteer to read aloud Mark 7:21–22. Direct members to respond to the first activity in the *Rethink* section of the Study Guide. Play the video clip for Lesson 6. Call for volunteers to suggest some possible reasons for our inability to live within God's basic principles. List responses on the board. Point out that our awareness of the Holy Spirit's presence and direction in our lives causes us to make decisions based on our own reasoning. That is the root of poor thinking and bad decision-making.

1. A NEW PERSPECTIVE (2 CORINTHIANS 5:16). Paul said "from now on." This signifies a change had taken place. The change was the salvation experience. Regarding people "according to the flesh" is phrased in *The Message* as evaluating "people by what they have or how they look." Paul pointed out that some people experienced Jesus in the flesh only; that is, they knew he existed but refused to acknowledge his divinity.

Discuss the difficulty of evaluating people according to God's perspective. Point out that we still have the tendency to evaluate people in this way. Discuss some ways to prevent evaluating people according to the worldly standards.

2. A NEW CREATION (2 CORINTHIANS 5:17). If possible, bring to the class some modeling clay and reflect on this verse while you create a ball or square with the clay. Ask a volunteer to read the

verse aloud and, as the phrase "new creation" is spoken, smash the sculpture and begin crafting a different item with the clay.

Point out that the idea of a new creation doesn't mean that the old creation gets a new coat of paint; it means the old creation is destroyed and a new way of life is begun. Being transformed into the likeness of Christ means life is no longer the way it once was. List on the board some things that are changed when the Holy Spirit takes over a person's life.

3. A NEW RESPONSIBILITY (2 CORINTHIANS 5:18–21). It's not all about us! Being changed by the Holy Spirit is just the beginning of the Christian experience. In verse 18, Paul refers to our new responsibility as the "ministry of reconciliation." Reconciliation targets two relationships—the relationship with God and the relationships with other people. The fact is, these two are sequential and repetitive. They are sequential in that we cannot be reconciled to others until we are reconciled to God. They are repetitive in that we are constantly renewing our relationship with God as we grow spiritually.

Discuss some ways that a person's faith in God affects his or her relationship with other people. Be prepared to address the idea that some relationships are negatively affected by a person's conversion experience. These relationships usually are the relationships we have with people who are not believers. We must be careful not to compromise our faith in order to maintain relationships like these.

Sometimes we get it all wrong—we try to fix broken interpersonal relationships without considering our relationship with God. When the Holy Spirit takes over control of our lives, we are remade and recommissioned for God's purposes. This is the path to a life of peace and purpose. We can only find real peace when we live to do those things for which God has designed us.

Making It Real: Ask volunteers to identify what they think of when they consider the concept of the good life. List responses on the board. Direct members to complete the activity in the *React* section of the Study Guide. Then read the following quote from the Study Guide:

"Are you living life with a new heart? Are you seeing things from a godly perspective? If so, you can testify about God's power to change a person's life. If not, you have yet to accept Jesus's invitation to live in his life; you are not yet "in Christ." This isn't a game show where you can hope you're right; this is the difference between life with Christ or life without Christ. It's a decision that has present and eternal implications."

Close with prayer.

CHAPTER 7: HEAVEN'S "WHOEVER" POLICY

Scripture Focus: Luke 16:19–31

Lesson Objective: To discover that no one is excluded from God's offer of salvation and to commit to extending the offer to everyone we encounter.

Before the small group session read Chapter 7 of 3:16.

The Context: As Jesus approached Jerusalem where he would eventually die, he addressed a variety of issues with his disciples. One of those issues was the idea that heaven was reserved for those who deserved it. Among the Jewish hierarchy, there was the belief that a person's importance on earth would translate into heavenly importance. To combat that concept, Jesus told the story of the rich man and Lazarus. Lazarus was the name of the friend Jesus raised from the dead, but there is no evidence that Jesus's use of the name here is in reference to his friend.

Getting Started: Enlist a volunteer to read aloud Luke 16:19–31. Take a few moments to establish the context for this passage.

Discovering the Truth: Direct members to respond to the first activity in the *Rethink* section of the Study Guide. Discuss the reasons God wants a relationship with his people. The primary reason God wants this relationship is because of his unending love for us. Play the video clip for Lesson 7. Write on the board "rich man" and "Lazarus." Explain that our ideas about the requirements for entrance into heaven align us with one of the men in this story; there are no other choices.

1. WHICH WAY? (LUKE 16:19–23). It is easy to fall into the trap of believing that our accomplishments on earth will mean something when we get to heaven. The rich man was clothed in purple—a sign of royalty or riches. Purple dye was expensive, so those who wore purple were declaring to the world their wealth. Ask the class to reflect on things we do in order to announce our societal positions. Lazarus, on the other hand, was left at the mercy of the rich man. Lazarus obviously had some problems that made him physically unattractive. His sores were subject to infection because the dogs licked them. As a beggar, he was dependent upon the generosity of those who felt compassion on him. By the world's standards, the rich man was fit for heaven. By God's standards, Lazarus was heaven-bound. Point out that God's standards, not man's, determine who gets into heaven.

2. A DAY LATE (LUKE 16:24–26). Lazarus traded his life of

misery for the comfort of Abraham in heaven. The rich man traded his comfort on earth for the misery of eternity in hell. The rich man's realization that he had made a mistake came too late. When the rich man pleaded with Abraham, there was nothing that could be done. There is a great gulf that separates heaven from hell and the gulf cannot be crossed after death.

Discuss some of the reasons people delay their decisions to accept Jesus as Lord and Savior. Be sure to make yourself available to those who might have questions about their salvation.

3. THE HARD REALITY (LUKE 16:27–31). The rich man's fate couldn't be affected, so he begged Abraham to send Lazarus to warn his family members of their need to accept God's grace. Abraham told the rich man that his brothers had access to Scripture and that was all they needed. The rich man countered by arguing that his brothers would believe if they saw someone return from the dead. Abraham's words serve as a warning to everyone—if people don't believe the Scripture, they aren't going to believe that someone rose from the dead.

Discuss the importance of believing the biblical revelation that reveals God's love, grace, and mercy. Remind the class that they have people in their lives that need to be warned about their eternal destination before it's too late.

Salvation comes to those who trust God, not to those who trust their own accomplishments. There is nothing we can do to earn salvation; it is God's gift. We accept it through faith—faith that has no socioeconomic boundaries.

Making It Real: Write on the board "stumbling block" and then call for a volunteer to read aloud Matthew 18:6–7. Point out that our individual freedom ends when it begins to negatively affect other people. Call for class members to suggest situations that might cause others to stumble. Based on this passage, causing others to stumble is a serious transgression.

Close with prayer.

CHAPTER 8: BELIEVE AND RECEIVE

Scripture Focus: 1 John 1:1–10

Lesson Objective: To discover the true meaning of faith and to commit to living in a faith-based relationship with God.
Before the small group session read Chapter 8 of *3:16*.

The Context: John's letter addresses the problems that were being caused by teachers who misrepresented God's grace. John, because of his personal relationship with Jesus Christ, was in a position to set the story straight. He knew Jesus personally, so his information was more accurate than second-hand information from people who really didn't know Jesus.

Getting Started: Enlist a volunteer to read aloud 1 John 1:1–10. Take a few moments to establish the context for this passage.

Discovering the Truth: Play the video clip for Lesson 8. Direct members to respond to the first activity in the *Rethink* section of the Study Guide. Discuss some of the things we take as true but lack evidence to legitimize our beliefs. List some examples on the board.

1. WHAT HAVE YOU SEEN (1 JOHN 1:1–4)? In a trial, witnesses are called upon to testify about those things they know to

be true. Attorneys will grill witnesses to make sure that their testimony is fact-based, not speculation. In John's time, people who were recognized as teachers were dispensing information that did not match what John knew to be true. Therefore, he began his letter by reminding his readers that his words weren't speculation, they reflected his eyewitness account of his personal experience with Jesus.

Discuss some of the things that class members have experienced in their spiritual lives. Point out that discussing these things is something that will serve as an encouragement to others.

2. WHAT DOES IT MEAN (1 JOHN 1:5–7)? It is one thing to know about Jesus; it's another thing to allow the Holy Spirit to live in and through you. That's what John said in this portion of the passage. John wasn't altering the message; he was passing along what he heard and saw. John proposed that faith and life are connected. Therefore, saying that you believe but living as if you don't is evidence that you don't really have a relationship with Jesus Christ.

Discuss some of the ways a person's faith should affect different aspects of his or her daily life. List responses on the board.

3. WHEN IS IT REAL (1 JOHN 1:8–10)? The first step to faith in God is expressing the truth about ourselves. John said that we lie if we claim to have no sin. But that confessing our sins puts us in a position to accept God's forgiveness. Sin is judged against God's criteria, not against the performances of other people.

Discuss the criteria by which we determine sin. How does our criteria compare to God's criteria?

Being in a faith-based relationship with God means living his way, by his rules. When our lives fail to match up with what we claim to believe, we must investigate the cause and make sure we really have a faith-based relationship with him.

Making It Real: Direct class members to work through the *React* section of the Study Guide. Discuss the questions in the activity and carefully review the meaning of 1 John 1:9. Remind the class that real faith is realized in our daily lives in the ways that we treat people we encounter in our homes, workplaces, and the community.

Close with prayer.

CHAPTER 9: GOD'S GRACIOUS GRIP

Scripture Focus: John 10:22–30

Lesson Objective: To discover the permanence of salvation and to commit to living with confidence in God's power to keep us in his grip.
Before the small group session read Chapter 9 of 3:16.

The Context: The Gospel of John was written to show people how to find eternal life. The opening verse connects the present to the very beginning—creation. It moves forward in the way that a seasoned attorney plots a case. Chapter 10 often is referred to as The Shepherd's Discourse. In this conversation, Jesus separates himself from any other way to eternal life. He told his followers how to experience the abundant life (v. 10) and then spoke to them about the permanence of their relationship with God.

Getting Started: Enlist a volunteer to read aloud John 10:22–30. Take a few moments to establish the context for this passage.

Discovering the Truth: Direct members to respond to the first activity in the *Rethink* section of the Study Guide. Point out that it is important to believe that one's salvation is permanent because it affects every area of life. Discuss the effect of salvation being conditional. It is safe to say that people who believe their salvation can be lost become ineffective as disciples because their concern is not for the spiritual well-being of others, but for themselves.

1. THE TROUBLING CONCERN (JOHN 10:22–24). The Jews expected a military leader who would assert Jewish superiority and reaffirm them as God's chosen people. Even though Jesus fulfilled Old Testament prophecy, the Jews didn't want to believe in him because he preached "whosoever" salvation. The Jews wanted to doubt him, even though everything they saw contradicted their doubts. They wanted Jesus to say plainly, "I am the Messiah." Why? It wasn't so they could worship him, but so they could charge him with blasphemy and put him to death.

What are some reasons that people today doubt the credibility of Jesus and his Word? What can we do to show them that God's Word is true and that Jesus is who he claimed to be?

2. AN UNPOPULAR RESPONSE (JOHN 10:25). Jesus explained that there was more than enough evidence to support his claim of being God's Son. Those who didn't believe chose not to believe because they wanted salvation on their terms.

Discuss some of the terms that often are a part of a person's desire for salvation. Why is it popular to believe that salvation happens through negotiation?

3. THE TRUTH REVEALED (JOHN 10:26–30). Jesus pointed out that there was an obvious reason that the Jews didn't understand what he was talking about—they didn't have a faith-based relationship with him. Those who have that kind of relationship

understood what Jesus was talking about. The Jews didn't want to believe; they wanted to discredit him.

In this passage, Jesus spoke about the permanence of salvation. Twice he said that no one can take away salvation from those who have genuinely experienced it. If that statement was true then, it remains true now. Discuss some reasons people believe they can lose their salvation. What Scriptures are used to support their belief?

If salvation is temporary, it isn't salvation. When we are saved, we are permanently granted access to heaven. We still face judgment and still will have to answer for those times when we have failed him. To believe that salvation can be lost is to say that Jesus's words in this passage were untrue!

Making It Real: Play the video clip for Lesson 9. Direct class members to work through the *React* section of the Study Guide.

Close with prayer.

CHAPTER 10: HELL'S SUPREME SURPRISE

Scripture Focus: Matthew 7:13–23

Lesson Objective: To discover the seriousness of hell and to commit to living with the desire to warn as many as possible of hell's ugliness.
Before the small group session read Chapter 10 of 3:16.

The Context: One of Jesus's most famous discourses is the Sermon on the Mount (Matthew 5:1–7:29). The content for this lesson is part of Jesus's warnings (Matthew 7:13–27). By being at the end of the sermon, these words would be some of the most vivid in the minds of those who heard him speak. For that reason, these words are of major significance.

Getting Started: Enlist a volunteer to read aloud Matthew 7:13–23. Take a few moments to establish the context for this passage.

Discovering the Truth: Direct members to respond to the first activity in the *Rethink* section of the Study Guide. Write "hell" on the board and call for volunteers to suggest some words that come to mind when they hear the word. List responses on the board.

1. THE NARROW WAY (MATTHEW 7:13–14). Fortified cities had limited access. Many of the passages into the city were barely large enough for a person to fit through. This was intentional. A soldier from an enemy army couldn't make it through the gate with his spear and shield. Getting in the gate was reserved for those who carried nothing. Reflect on this fact in light of Jesus's words regarding the narrow way. Many people still believe that they will take to heaven their possessions and accomplishments. Jesus pointed out that all of those things will be left behind when a person stands before God.

Discuss some of the "baggage" that keeps people from a meaningful relationship with God. Spend some time reflecting on the concept of faith and how it is independent of a person's wealth, popularity, appearance, or accomplishments.

2. THE FRUITFUL LIFE (MATTHEW 7:15–18). How can a person know if his or her faith is authentic? Jesus offered a test—look at the fruit. We must be careful to apply this evaluation to ourselves before applying it to others. We are good at ignoring our own

shortcomings while criticizing others for theirs. Discuss some of the things that people do that are valuable to God's kingdom. Discuss some things we think are valuable but are, in fact, worthless.

3. THE TRAGIC ASSUMPTION (MATTHEW 7:21–23). Knowing about Jesus and knowing Jesus are two different things. Jesus warned his audience not to fall into the trap of believing they were saved by trusting something other than a faith-based relationship with him.

Many people who are affiliated with the church do not share the foundational faith of those who are legitimate followers of Jesus Christ. Remind class members that their first responsibility is to watch and guard their own lives. We are never to become the Holy Spirit for other people.

It is tragic to go through life with faith that is built on family history, religious affiliation, or misconceived criteria. Yet many people today do that very thing. They believe they will get into heaven because they are good, religious, and related to other people of faith. This is the tragedy about which Jesus spoke.

Making It Real: Play the video clip for Lesson 10. Direct class members to work through the *React* section of the Study Guide.

Close with prayer.

CHAPTER 11: WHAT MAKES HEAVEN HEAVENLY

Scripture Focus: Revelation 21:1–26

Lesson Objective: To discover the awesomeness of heaven and to commit to living in this life as a resident of heaven.

Before the small group session read Chapter 11 of 3:16.

The Context: John's revelation while on the island of Patmos is one of the most controversial books in the Bible. The descriptions make it obvious that John was using figurative language to describe what he saw. Therefore, without concrete descriptions, John's meaning often is unclear. The final two chapters describe the new heaven and the new earth that will be in place following Christ's return. This new heaven and new earth serves as an encouragement to everyone who labors for the cause of Christ.

Getting Started: Play the video clip for Lesson 11. Enlist volunteers to read aloud Revelation 21:1–26. Take a few moments to establish the context for this passage.

Discovering the Truth: Direct members to respond to the first activity in the *Rethink* section of the Study Guide. Ask members to explain why they would or would not choose to live in a perfect world. Then call for members to share their concepts of heaven. List key words on the board.

1. REMADE (REVELATION 21:1–5). Ever since the sin of Adam and Eve, the earth has been under God's curse. Satan was called the prince of the earth. Evil has been the norm and pleasing God a struggle. But, when Christ returns, everything changes. Heaven and earth will be remade and some of the things we have grown accustomed to will be gone.

Review the passage and list on the board the things that will no longer be a part of our existence. Call for volunteers to share ways they have experienced some of these painful and trying things. Ask them to reflect on the feelings they have knowing that all of the pain and sorrow of life will disappear.

2. RECLAIMED (REVELATION 21:6–8). Eternal punishment awaits those who have lifestyles characterized by the things listed in verse 8. God will reclaim his world and those who live in opposition to him will be cast into eternal punishment—hell. This is referred to as the second death. The first death was physical and the second will be spiritual. The first death was temporary in nature and the second will be permanent. Death often is viewed as final. The second death will be eternally final! Review verse 8 and point out that Christians today are affected by these things. Call for volunteers to suggest things that believers can do in order to minimize the effect of these things in their lives.

3. REJUVENATED (REVELATION 21:22–26). There will be no temple in the new city because the worship of God will be the only activity of its inhabitants. Faith will no longer be compartmentalized to a day or a place; worshiping God will be the totality of our existence. Light will be radiated from God's existence.

Discuss what people think living in heaven will be like. What will be the same as our lives now? What will be different?

The very concept of heaven makes some people skeptical of the life of faith. They can't comprehend a place where there will be no pain, suffering, crime, or disappointment. Some believe they will be bored with the constant praise of God. But, what is the other option? Eternal punishment in hell!

Making It Real: Direct class members to work through the *React* section of the Study Guide.

Close with prayer.

CHAPTER 12: THE LAST WORD ON LIFE

Scripture Focus: 1 Peter 1:3–12

Lesson Objective: To discover the hope that God provides and to commit to living in light of his hope.
Before the small group session read Chapter 12 of 3:16.

The Context: The apostle Peter is credited with the authorship of the epistles that bear his name. Peter wrote at a time when Christians were being persecuted by the Roman government. Peter would eventually lose his life as punishment for being a Christ-follower. He wrote to encourage believers who might have cause to lose hope. His words are practical advice for every believer.

Getting Started: Enlist volunteers to read aloud 1 Peter 1:3–12. Take a few moments to establish the context for this passage.

Discovering the Truth: Direct members to respond to the first activity in the *Rethink* section of the Study Guide. List on the board some things that people can count on and then discuss why those things are trusted.

1. LIVING HOPE (1 PETER 1:3–5). The hope for believers isn't a dead hope. Our hope isn't in a dead leader or the legacy of a historical figure. Our hope is a living hope that results from our relationship with Jesus Christ. Peter recognized that salvation was a result of God's mercy, not deserved by anyone.

Review the passage and call for volunteers to share their

thoughts about living hope. Discuss ways in which one's hope is shared with others.

2. TEMPORARY TRIALS (1 PETER 1:6–9). Call for volunteers to share some of the trials they experience on an ongoing basis. List responses on the board. Peter pointed out that the trials we encounter are temporary and might even cloud one's ability to see God clearly, but we can be sure that God is there with us every step of the way. What really matters is that we are destined for eternity with God in heaven.

3. INCREDIBLE FUTURE (1 PETER 1:10–12). The salvation we have is the very thing that people have been searching for throughout history. Call for volunteers to share some experiences when the hype about an activity was more impressive than the activity. Point out that the promise of heaven is something that we might never understand, but provides lasting hope for every day.

Life is a choice—heaven or hell. The choice affects every aspect of life both now and for eternity. We must never minimize this decision. It is something that must be taken seriously.

Making It Real: Play the video clip for Lesson 12. Direct class members to work through the *React* section of the Study Guide. As the class concludes, read the following quote from *3:16*.

"Jesus has been to Bethlehem, wearing barn rags and hearing sheep crunch. Suckling milk and shivering against the cold. All of divinity content to cocoon itself in an eight-pound body and to sleep on a cow's supper. Millions who face the chill of empty pockets or the fears of sudden change turn to Christ. Why?

"Because he's been there.

"He's been to Nazareth, where he made deadlines and paid

bills; to Galilee, where he recruited direct reports and separated fighters; to Jerusalem, where he stared down critics and stood up against cynics.

"We have our Nazareths as well—demands and due dates. Jesus wasn't the last to build a team; accusers didn't disappear with Jerusalem's temple. Why seek Jesus's help with your challenges? Because he's been there. To Nazareth, to Galilee, to Jerusalem.

"But most of all, he's been to the grave. Not as a visitor, but as a corpse. Buried amidst the cadavers. Numbered among the dead. Heart silent and lungs vacant. Body wrapped and grave sealed. The cemetery. He's been buried there."

Close with prayer.